EMBRACE YOUR
SKIN COLOR

QUEANA MITCHELL

Copyright © 2023 by Queana Mitchell

EMBRACE YOUR SKIN COLOR

All rights reserved. No part of this publication may be reproduced, distributed, or transmitted in any form or by any means, including photocopying, recording, or other electronic or mechanical methods, without the prior written permission of the publisher, except in the case of brief quotations embodied in critical reviews and certain other noncommercial uses permitted by copyright law. For permission requests, write to the publisher, addressed "Attention: Permissions Coordinator," at info@beyondpublishing.net

Quantity sales and special discounts are available on quantity purchases by corporations, associations, and others. For details, contact the publisher at the address above.

Orders by U.S. trade bookstores and wholesalers. Email info@ BeyondPublishing.net

The Beyond Publishing Speakers Bureau can bring authors to your live event. For more information or to book an event contact the Beyond Publishing Speakers Bureau speak@BeyondPublishing.net

The Author can be reached directly at BeyondPublishing.net

Manufactured and printed in the United States of America distributed globally by BeyondPublishing.net

New York | Los Angeles | London | Sydney

ISBN Softcover: 978-1-63792-568-3
ISBN Hardcover: 978-1-63792-566-9

John 14:6
Jesus saith unto him, I am the way, the truth, and the life: no man cometh unto the Father, but by me.

Psalm 18:30-32 KJV
[30] As for God, his way is perfect: the word of the Lord is tried: he is a buckler to all those that trust in him. [31] For who is God save the Lord ? or who is a rock save our God? [32] It is God that girdeth me with strength and maketh my way perfect.

TABLE OF CONTENTS

Chapter 1   Tiffany Introduction 7

Chapter 2   Tiffany Greeted Amber 9

Chapter 3   Amber Show Tiffany Around the House 12

Chapter 4   Amber Life Turn Upside Down 16

Chapter 5   Tiffany Set up Amber 22

Chapter 6   Jane Comfort Amber 31

Chapter 7   Everything Turns Out Great for Amber but for Tiffany not that all Great 38

Self-Love Poem 42

Prayer 49

Psalm 86:11 KJV
[11] *Teach me thy way, O Lord ;*
I will walk in thy truth: unite my heart to fear thy name.

Philippians 4:11-13 KJV
[11] *Not that I speak in respect of want: for I have learned,*
in whatsoever state I am, therewith to be content.
[12] *I know both how to be abased, and I know how to*
abound: everywhere and in all things
I am instructed both to be full and to be hungry,
both to abound and to suffer need.
[13] *I can do all things through*
Christ which strengtheneth me.

CHAPTER 1

TIFFANY INTRODUCTION

Hey, my name is Ms. Mitchell and I'm 25 years old, and I decided to write a book to help women across the world. I talked to some young teenage girls and also grown women, to learn about their skin color and how they feel about their skin. At first, I was doubtful and scared to ask the questions; I didn't know how well women will receive my question. If they are going to take it personally or not, I still made an effort to ask them.

I did all this because I was concerned about women and young teens that do not feel good about themselves. I'm so tired of hearing 'My skin is too dark, it has to be lighter', 'my skin is too white it has to be darker' or 'I have a skin disorder and people make fun of me'. So, what if your skin is darker, brighter, or different? Don't change your skin color for anybody; don't do it because no one is ever worth changing your identity for. You are wasting your time. Be the young or older independent woman that you are and motivate yourself through your struggles and pain.

Don't let your low esteem or lack of confidence ever bring you down. And do not say that you are not strong enough because you are, you just haven't realized it yet but trust me you will get there.

Your life wasn't meant to be perfect. You may go through some bumps here and there, but you are still here. You still have time to make things right. Life is so hard, but it is up to you to push through your obstacles. Yes, you may come across people who hate you or do not like you, that prey on your weaknesses, but you have to be tough, no matter what challenge you have to face.

I talked to a young lady named Tiffany who is 19 years old now and was born in Atlanta, Georgia. She told me how she experienced low esteem at a point in her life and never thought she was good enough to achieve much in life. Now she regrets it all, but there was a time when she believed it.

For the longest time possible, I wondered why she would say that. I paused and pondered why but I had no answer until Tiffany continued with her story. She recalled that when she was in 7th grade in junior high school, she saw a girl, Amber. She was the same age as Tiffany, but her skin issue made her stand out. Tiffany saw this as an opportunity to start teasing Amber. Although Tiffany knew that Amber was born with a skin disorder and couldn't help it, Tiffany still didn't stop teasing her.

Amber was a beautiful young lady with brown eyes and long, silky black hair. Amber was just perfect, but her skin was the issue. Even Tiffany thought that she was beautiful, but she was jealous of Amber's beauty. Tiffany didn't realize that she had low self-esteem herself, which prevented her from acknowledging the fact that she envied Amber.

CHAPTER 2

TIFFANY GREETED AMBER

One day, Tiffany and her friends walked up to Amber and greeted her but Amber was so closed off and shy, she didn't reply to their pleasant greeting.

Tiffany talked to her for a while and eventually, convinced Amber for a school tour. Tiffany and her friends showed her around the school since it was Amber's first time at this school. She even invited Amber over to her place after school, but Amber didn't accept. Tiffany tried her best to persuade Amber to come. It wasn't hard because somehow, Tiffany always got her way with people.

Amber finally said yes and was over the moon. She had never had a friend in her life, which made her appreciate Tiffany's friendship even more. When Amber was a little girl, she was bullied at school and none of her schoolmates wanted to be around her. They teased her for her skin color and always told her that it was horrible. Some even used to say they feel like throwing up when they see Amber. The poor girl had been through too much, but she still pushed through all the pain and hurt. And then she met Tiffany.

And thought that things would finally change for the better, unaware that Tiffany was just another bully waiting for a chance to destroy Amber's life.

As agreed, Amber went to Tiffany's house on Friday night. She met Tiffany's parents and they were pleased to meet her. After they had eaten, Tiffany invited Amber to her room. It was a sight to behold and Amber was so shocked to see the huge room. Amber always wished for a room like that but she knew some dreams were just not meant to be.

When Tiffany showed Amber her makeup collection, Amber got excited too. Suddenly, Tiffany got an idea and wanted to do a makeover for Amber, but Amber hesitated. She didn't want to because even though she loved makeup, her lack of confidence always stopped her from applying any. But Tiffany had some tricks up her sleeves and again she convinced Amber, who didn't suspect Tiffany's intentions at all.

The girls gathered all the makeup stuff they needed, and Tiffany also took out some of her clothes.

Tiffany went the extra mile and dressed up Amber. She even styled Amber's hair. The result was stunning because Amber looked gorgeous. She looked in **the mirror and couldn't believe how amazing she looked. She beamed with happiness and kept staring at her reflection. But Tiffany had quite a different expression on her face. She looked at Amber with a frown, as her heart filled with jealousy and hate. She did like Amber, but her beauty was something Tiffany couldn't tolerate. The day ended with Amber leaving home, thanking Tiffany for the makeover. After she left, all Tiffany could do was lie in her bed, fuming over her stupidity.**

On Sunday morning, Amber invited Tiffany to come to church with her and Tiffany agreed. She enjoyed it, and after the services were over, the pastor came up to preach the Lord's words. The day's sermon was about jealousy and hatred, and that had a wonderful message at the end. Tiffany sat there listening, and some of the preacher's words touched her heart.

He said, *"Jealousy and hate are not of God. It is from the enemy, so if you are jealous and hateful towards someone's beauty and success, you are blocking the blessings that God has in store for you. Oh So, stop wasting your time on someone else success and beauty, focus on your success and beauty".*

Tiffany stood up and clapped hard, and she suddenly realized that the message was for her. Once the service was over, Amber took Tiffany to her house for Sunday brunch. All of Amber's family was there and Tiffany had never felt so welcome. Although Tiffany lived in a big house and had rich parents, she had always missed something in her life. And at that moment, surrounded by people who loved and supported each other, Tiffany realized what was missing from her life. It was family. Amber had love and loyalty from her family, something that Tiffany had only dreamt of.

Amber also introduced Tiffany to her parents, which didn't go as she had planned. Amber's dad liked Tiffany and was very polite. But when Tiffany met Amber's mom, she found her to be cold and unimpressed. The sentiments were mutual because Amber's mom also didn't like Tiffany. She had a feeling that there was something off about Tiffany, which made her cautious.

CHAPTER 3

AMBER SHOW TIFFANY AROUND THE HOUSE

Tiffany ignored the unease and followed Amber around the house. She was surprised to see that although the house wasn't as big and elegant as hers, it was still stunning. The simplicity of it all made Tiffany fall in love with the house, something she never thought was possible. Even Amber's small and simple room looked better!

The two girls talked for hours about life and the future they were planning. But soon, Tiffany steered the conversation toward guys and asked Amber if she had ever had a boyfriend. Amber said no and smiled shyly.

Tiffany saw Amber's expression and paused for a second. She told Amber that she wanted to hook her up with a boy. Amber quickly said no, but then Tiffany calmed her down by saying that the boy was her boyfriend's friend, Daniel.

As usual, Amber was quite adamant about not doing anything that would end her in trouble.

But Tiffany wasn't having any of it and persisted. Amber's resolve quickly broke because she also wanted to know how it

felt like to have a boyfriend, and she said yes. Tiffany smiled at Amber, but she was laughing inside because she had an evil plan in mind. Tiffany soon went home, as she plotted how to embarrass Amber.

With Tiffany gone, Amber's mother called her into the living room to talk. As Amber sat down, her mother's words shocked her. She clearly explained that she didn't trust Amber's friend and it was better if Amber too stayed away from her.

Amber was surprised, but she knew she had to defend her friend, and that's what she did. Amber asked her mother the reason for her distrust, but she had no answer. Amber tried to explain that Tiffany hadn't done anything wrong and was her best friend.

But Amber's mother replied that despite everything, she still didn't trust, Tiffany and wanted Amber to stay away from her. She could feel that Tiffany was trouble and knew that Amber could do without her easily. Amber, on the other hand, didn't see things the same way. She got mad at her mother and screamed that she would continue to talk to Tiffany because there was nothing anyone could do to stop her.

Amber's father heard the commotion and ran downstairs to see what had happened. It would have become a messy argument, but Amber's mother didn't want that. So, she tried to pacify the situation and said, *"It is just a misunderstanding, nothing else. Come on, honey, let's go to bed. We have a long day ahead of us."*

The next day, Amber felt guilty for misbehaving with her mother. She had raised her voice and screamed at her mother for the first time and she was mad at herself now. But she also hoped that her mother would forgive her. These things were still on her mind when she entered school. But as soon as she saw Tiffany's friends standing there, she forgot everything her mother had said and ran to meet them.

But the girls had other plans. As soon as they saw Amber, they started making fun of her in front of everybody. Unable to understand what was going on and unable to endure any more bullying, Amber ran to the bathroom, sobbing. She didn't even know that Tiffany was behind it all.

Soon Tiffany went to the bathroom and saw Amber crying there. Acting all nice, she asked what.

What had happened to make Amber so upset the poor, unsuspecting girl explained everything to Tiffany.

With tears flowing down her face, Amber said, *"People only see me as a punching bag. I am nobody!"*

Tiffany was secretly happy but had to play a part, so she tried to console Amber.

"You are special, and you are somebody. Never set yourself up for failure."

Amber heard the encouraging words from her friend and reached out to hug her. When the storm of emotions subsided, Amber felt a lot better. Tiffany gave her some tissues to wipe her face and told her to get up.

"I have a big surprise for you, after school," Tiffany said.

"You're the best friend I've ever had!" Amber said, unaware of the cruel surprise that was in store for her.

So, Amber and Tiffany both walked out of the bathroom and went to class. When the school bell rang at the end of the day, Amber went out to meet.

Tiffany, who was waiting for her outside. Amber saw Tiffany standing there with a boy as she walked up to her.

Tiffany introduced Daniel, and Amber was so nervous she couldn't believe it. It was exciting but also terrifying for Amber and she started shaking. Seeing how nervous Amber was, Tiffany left the two alone and walked away. Daniel and Amber talked for a while and got to know each other more.

Just a few minutes were enough to help Amber calm down. Soon she was on cloud nine. Daniel walked her home and on the way to her house, they talked some more. Amber felt her initial hesitation slowly ebbing away. Daniel told her it was nice meeting her and Amber said the same. As they reached her house, Daniel kissed her on her cheek and Amber was blown away. They both said goodbye and Amber walked into the house. That is when she saw her mother on the living room floor.

Amber ran to check up on her and didn't see her breathing. She quickly called 911 and thankfully, the paramedics arrived within a few minutes. By then, Amber had called her dad too, who arrived home.

CHAPTER 4

AMBER LIFE TURN UPSIDE DOWN

Few minutes after the paramedics. They reached the hospital and Amber's mom was rushed to the emergency ward, while she and her dad waited outside, praying for her speedy recovery. They waited to hear from the doctor, but when they finally came out, the news wasn't good.

"I'm sorry, but she didn't make it." And these words changed everything for Amber. She hugged her dad and cried with him. They were both lost and had no clue what to do next. But the news got even worse.

The doctors concluded that Amber's mom died because of blood loss, which also caused the death of her unborn child. Yes! She was pregnant at the time and didn't even know it. Amber and her father were also unaware of this. The news made the loss even greater, as now they had two lives to mourn.

Once they were back home, a drained Amber ran upstairs to her room crying. She regretted every unkind word that she had ever said to her mom, but most of all, she was appalled by her behavior towards her mom recently. Every night after the death of her mom, Amber had nightmares. Every night she would pray to God to protect and heal her and her father.

Ever since the death of his wife, Amber's dad had started drinking. It worried Amber a lot and made her sick to see her father this way. She never wanted her father to be an alcoholic and she tried her best to stop him.

Every day she asked him, *"Why do you drink so much?"*

And he'd answer, *"I have lots of pain in my heart. I drink to get some peace."*

Amber felt sorry for her dad, but there wasn't much she could do to help him. She didn't know that soon his drinking habit would become a part of their life.

With so much going on at home, Amber tried to find some solace at school. But even that didn't work. On a Tuesday morning, Amber arrived at school to see Tiffany kissing Daniel in front of the whole school. At first, Amber couldn't believe her eyes, but soon she felt embarrassed and ashamed. She turned away, unable to see the sight before her eyes. She had trusted Tiffany and that is how she had repaid her.

Suddenly the words of her mother rang in her ears. *"Tiffany, she is not to be trusted."* And Amber's mother was right all along.

Amber walked right past Tiffany and went to class. The day went by in a daze and once the final bell rang, Amber went straight to her locker. There she saw an invitation to Tiffany's birthday party on Friday night. At first, she didn't want to go, but she wanted to confront Tiffany about the whole situation, about Daniel and her friendship.

Amber went home and took a relaxing shower to calm her nerves. Once done, she cooked food for herself and her father.

She didn't feel like eating, but she knew she had to. So, she forced herself to eat a few bites and was done within minutes.

Her father was still slumped at the table and Amber got busy washing the dishes. And that's when she felt her father standing right behind her. Before she could turn around, he hugged her and started kissing her neck.

Amber was in shock and told her father to stop, but he didn't let her go. He pulled down his pants and hiked up her dress.

That's when Amber realized what was about to happen and she started screaming. Her father clapped a hand on her mouth, muffling her screams as he raped her. She wanted to cry out from the searing pain, but he held her down.

It didn't last long but it seemed like a lifetime to Amber, who was pinned on the floor. Her father stood up, still stumbling but satisfied now. He threw alcohol at her and told her she was a nobody. Amber cried but was thankful the ordeal was over. She ran up to her room, locked the door, and covered herself with her bedsheets.

The next morning, Amber called Jane, the pastor's wife, and asked her if she would let Amber stay over. Jane wanted to know why, so Amber told her everything. At first. Jane could not believe her ears, but the pain in Amber's voice confirmed her story.

Jane said that she'd pick Amber up in the afternoon. Amber was grateful for the kind gesture and she started packing quickly. She also cleaned up her room and wrote a note for her dad. As she had promised, Jane arrived in the afternoon and helped Amber get all her stuff in the car.

On her way out of the door, Amber stuck her note in the mailbox, so her father could see it. Amber was in tears and wished her mom was still alive. Her life would have been so different, but Amber knew there was no use in dreaming. This was the reality of her life and it was better if she accepted it sooner.

Jane looked over at Amber and felt sorry for the young girl. Without saying another word, she drove Amber to her house. It was a huge house and Amber couldn't believe it. As they entered the house, Richard, the pastor, came to meet them. He seemed surprised to see Amber there with all her belongings and asked Jane.

"I will tell you everything you want to know when I get inside the house," Jane replied. She didn't want to say anything in front of Amber because she knew it would make her feel awkward. Richard understood and nodded. He helped them carry the bags inside and even carried them upstairs to a room.

Jane made Amber close her eyes as they walked into the room. When she finally opened her eyes, Amber was shocked to see how big her room was. The big comfy bed looked perfect and even had a few stuffed toys on it. Amber beamed as she looked around the room. Jane was also happy for Amber. She knew how much Amber had been through. First the bullying, then her mother's death, and now the rape. She just wanted Amber to have a better life.

That night, Jane cooked up some delicious food as a treat for Amber. Just the scent of the hot food made Amber impatient to dig into the food. She was too hungry, but she knew she had to wait. Richard said gracefully and thanked God for the food. As soon as he said Amen, Amber grabbed some food and shoved it in her mouth.

Jane and Richard saw her eat and smiled, happy that they were able to help. Amber looked like she had lost weight and Jane wanted her to eat everything she liked.

Later, when Jane was cleaning up, Amber tried to help but Jane wasn't having any of it. She ordered Amber to go to her room and get some rest.

But once there, Amber felt like taking a shower to relax. The bathroom was big and had everything that Amber ever needed. She quickly showered and wanted to fall asleep, but Jane was waiting for her outside.

"Can you please come downstairs for a moment? I have something to talk to you about."

Dreading the worst, Amber went downstairs and saw Richard and Jane going through some documents.

"Please read the paperwork and sign it," Jane said as she handed the documents to Amber.

Amber read the papers and her heart stopped. They were adoption papers! Jane and Richard wanted to adopt her.

"Are you sure about this? What will my father say?" Amber asked.

"We'll take care of it all. We've already talked to your father. He is ready to give up his rights and we'd be happy if you choose to be our daughter," Richard said.

"But why?" Amber asked, still not understanding what was going on.

"Because we cannot have children, Amber. And we'd like to call you our own," Jane explained.

Amber was shocked to hear that. She always thought that the pastor and his wife had children. But now she knew. And she had an important life decision in front of her.

Amber thought about her life and the happy memories she had with her mother and dad. She wanted that again, and besides, Amber had started feeling sorry for Richard and Jane. They couldn't have children and yet they were so kind to her. So, Amber made her decision and she signed the paperwork in front of them. Richard and Jane were so pleased, they hugged her and thanked her. Soon, she was in bed, thanking God for all the good things in her life and getting her a caring family.

On her way to school the next day, Amber saw her dad. He was driving his car and had a few women in the backseat. Amber watched them go by and kept thinking about what it meant. Her day was about to get worse. As soon as she reached school, she saw Tiffany and Daniel holding hands. Amber had enough, and she went right past them, ignoring them.

CHAPTER 5

TIFFANY SET UP AMBER

Display of affection. She went to her locker to get her books and stuff for class.

The classes for the day began and soon the principal announced that the honor list had been posted. Amber wasn't interested at first but hearing all the other students talking excitedly built up her interest too. As soon as the school bell rang for lunchtime, everybody ran outside to see the honor roll list. Amber didn't want to deal with the crowded halls, so she decided to wait till after school to check the honor roll list.

Amber was alone in the lunchroom and happily ate the leftovers from her dinner. She went back to class just to see Tiffany and Daniel there. She tried her best to ignore the two and concentrated on her work. The teacher entered and announced a surprise test. While the rest of the class groaned, Amber was happy about the distraction. And anyway, she had prepared for it. As soon as Amber got her test, she immediately started to put the answers in the missing blank space. Tiffany, on the other hand, had no idea what to write so she was trying her best to glance at someone's paper.

Everyone was soon done with their tests and the teacher collected them. While she asked the students to do some exercises from the book, she sat in the corner and graded their papers. Once done, she started calling out each student's name and announced their marks to the class.

When it was finally Amber's turn, she went to get her test paper and was shocked when the teacher announced that she had scored full marks. The teacher started clapping and asked the other students to clap for Amber too. With the whole class applauding for her, Amber went back to her seat with the paper in her hand. She was so happy; she wanted to jump and scream right there in the classroom. But she had to keep her cool in class, so she stayed still.

Because Amber had scored such great marks, the teacher announced that nobody in the class would get homework as a celebration. Everybody was excited to hear that except for Amber. She liked to work hard and never shied away from doing her best. She was ambitious, which made her even more determined in life.

Once the school bell rang and school was over, Amber rushed to her locker to get her books. She was in a hurry because she still hadn't seen the honor list. Amber was amazed to see her name on top of the honor roll list. Amber was so happy she could not believe it and was on cloud nine. She walked down the steps and saw Tiffany's friends standing in the corner but she didn't care. She just walked down and passed by them, ignoring them. But as soon as Amber walked past them, one of Tiffany's friends gave her the thumbs up and said congratulations. Amber was astonished at first, but she said thank you and moved on. Amber was shocked to hear one of Tiffany's friends congratulate her because they had only teased her before.

Amber was walking home when she remembered that Tiffany's birthday was the next day. So, she went down to the mall to get Tiffany a gift. Thinking hard about what to get her, Amber remembered the makeup collection that Tiffany had shown her. Knowing that Tiffany loved makeup, Amber decided to buy her a new makeup set to add to her collection.

Amber chose one of the most stylish sets, purchased it, and walked out of the mall, happy. That's when she saw Daniel in the car park. He was sitting in his car, apparently waiting for someone. Amber wondered if he was waiting for Tiffany, but she walked away, minding her own business. But just the thought of what Tiffany had done to her made her blood boil. She had tried to forgive her, but the anger and the feelings of betrayal were still there.

Amber ran all the way home and slammed the door as she rushed into her room. She wanted to speak to Richard and Jane and went downstairs, looking for them.

One look at Amber was enough to let Jane know that there was something wrong.

"Is everything all right, dear? What happened? I heard you slamming the door," Jane said as Amber sat beside her.

"Yes, everything is all right with me, but I have to tell you something," Amber said quietly.

Jane nodded and Amber told her about Tiffany's birthday and asked her for permission to go.

thought hard for a minute and Amber waited. Jane knew about Tiffany and what she had done, so she was worried about Amber.

"I'm not going to stay that long, so you don't have to be worried about me. I'll be just fine," Amber reassured her.

"Oh, Okay. Just be careful," Jane said with a smile.

Amber hugged her and ran to her room. The next day, she looked through all her clothes and couldn't find one thing that was pretty enough to wear to a birthday party. She was ready to give up and ditch the plan when she heard a knock on the door.

"Come in, please," Amber said.

Jane walked in and sat beside Amber on the bed.

"I want to give you something, Amber. I have something for you to wear. Just hold on. I'll get it for you, "Jane said.

Amber got excited and waited patiently as Jane went out of the room to get the dress.

soon and asked Amber to close her eyes. Amber did as ask and sat on the bed, excited to see the dress.

"You can open them now," Jane said.

As soon as Amber opened her eyes, she saw Jane holding up a wonderful dress. The dress was simple and classic, just breathtaking. Jane helped Amber try on the dress, and it fit her like a glove. Amber looked in the mirror and she couldn't believe how amazing she looked. Jane helped her put her clothes back in the closet and even styled Amber's hair in an elegant updo. Amber put on her shoes and some perfume too. When she was ready, she walked out of her room to show Jane the complete look.

But Jane had something more in store for her. She handed Amber a necklace that belonged to her grandmother. Amber was shocked to see how beautiful the necklace was, but she didn't feel comfortable borrowing it, and she told Jane.

"I can't take this. It is yours."

"It's okay. I want you to have it. You look so beautiful!" Jane said.

Amber was happy about Jane's generosity and gave her a big hug to say thank you. Now that she was all dolled up, Amber went downstairs, put on her coat, and went off. She walked to Tiffany's house and was surprised to see a crowd there. Tiffany was so popular that almost everyone from their school had turned up for the party. She heard loud music from the house and was a bit nervous, but she put on a brave face and walked in. As she walked in, she kept an eye on the crowd, looking for Tiffany. She wanted to give her the gift and confront her. She wanted to tell Tiffany how she felt about what her friend had done to her. But Tiffany was nowhere to be found.

Amber went inside the living room, hoping that she'd see Tiffany there, but the room was full of people partying. She sat on the living room couch moving from side to side to the beat of the music.

Meanwhile, Jennifer, one of Tiffany's friends, saw Amber on the living room couch and ran up the stairs to tell Tiffany that Amber had arrived. She burst open the door to Tiffany's bedroom and saw her having sex with Daniel. Tiffany got upset at the interruption and screamed at Jennifer to get out of the room.

Mortified at what she had walked into, Jennifer quickly shut the door and went downstairs to the kitchen. She saw a bottle of wine and opened it, pouring some for herself.

Upstairs, Tiffany took a shower and got dressed. She looked amazing and she knew it. She went downstairs to look for Jennifer and knew that she'd be found where the liquor was. Jennifer's dad suffered from a drinking addiction problem and Jennifer had learned the behavior from him. She found Jennifer with an almost empty bottle and asked her to stop.

"What did you want to tell me?" Tiffany asked.

"Amber is here and she's looking for you," Jennifer said drunkenly.

"What? What the hell is she doing here?"

Jennifer just shrugged her shoulders and Tiffany went into the living room to look for Amber, anger visible on her face. But Tiffany wanted to do something explosive and, in a few seconds, she came up with a plan. It was a bad plan and Tiffany loved it.

Tiffany called Daniel downstairs and told him the plan. He did not like it, as Tiffany had expected but she pleaded with him to do it.

"I don't want to do that! You know I like you, Tiff! You must be crazy. I can't do this. It's wrong!" Daniel said.

"You have to, Daniel. If you love me, do it!" Tiffany said and Daniel realized he had no other choice.

He finally agreed to follow the plan and the reason was that he appreciated how Tiffany had his back since he was young. Tiffany's parents had helped Daniel's parents out financially when they were on the edge of getting ruined. And the help had not ceased till they could stand on their own.

Even in her drunken state, Jennifer did not like the plan and told Tiffany. It did not take long for Tiffany to put her in her place.

"Are you sure you want me to tell your parents about your drinking problem? Or how about I just announce it to the whole school?" Tiffany warned and Jennifer knew she had to back off.

Meanwhile, Daniel went to the living room and saw Amber sitting on the couch, her body swinging to the beat of the music.

"Hi. How are you?" Daniel said as he approached Amber.

Amber did not pay any attention to him but Daniel wasn't about to give up. Daniel told Amber that he was sorry for hurting her and pleaded with her to talk to him.

"I'm sorry for hurting you. Can we please talk? I know I don't deserve it, but I want to apologize for my behavior," Daniel lied.

"Why are you here? Shouldn't you be with your girlfriend? Anyway, where is she? I've got a gift for her," Amber said, still not looking at him.

"She's in the bathroom, but don't worry. Let's go upstairs. Then you can give her the present. And all three of us can sit and talk too," Daniel said.

Amber thought hard and finally said yes because she wanted to know more about the situation between Daniel and Tiffany. She also wanted answers about why Tiffany tried to hook her up with Daniel when she already fancied him. So, Amber went upstairs with Daniel to talk about the situation so she can clear the air between Daniel and Tiffany. When Amber asked Daniel, he lied and said that Tiffany had played her.

"Tiffany doesn't like you and she was just trying to make you jealous. She knew that you never had a boyfriend. When Tiffany had kissed me, I was upset. Then I saw you leave and it hurt me because I know you were hurting too. I never wanted to hurt you. I'm sorry Amber can you please forgive me?" Daniel said.

Amber was crying by then and tears flowed down her face. She had a good soul and always saw the best in people, which is why she hugged Daniel and said, *"I forgive you, Daniel"*.

All this time, Tiffany was just outside the room, listening to the conversation. Knowing that her plan was working, Tiffany could not help but feel excited. She was silently laughing at how gullible Amber was.

Inside the room, Daniel held onto Amber. The hug got too awkward for her and she started to wiggle, trying to push Daniel away. But it was time for him to put Tiffany's plan to action and he started to touch Amber's body. His hand slid down her back, while the other one held onto her tightly.

"What are you doing? Get away from me!" Amber said loudly but Daniel held on.

He lifted her dress and started to kiss her belly. Amber was too shocked to believe what was happening to her. She started screaming for help, but the music was too loud. Her voice did not even leave the room. Suddenly, Tiffany walked into the room, with a video recorder in her hand. She had the cruelest smile on her face as she recorded Amber's anguished looks.

"Help me!" Amber screamed as Tiffany filmed Daniel molesting her.

His hands touched her everywhere as he pinned Amber beneath him. She tried to struggle and free herself, but it was no use. He held her hands above her head with one hand, while the other one grabbed at her body. And then he did the one thing Amber had never expected. He raped her!

Tiffany stood by and watched as Amber cried from the pain. Amber's suffering made her feel happy and she recorded every moment of it. She was careful not to capture Daniel's face and only focused on Amber.

When Daniel was done, he and Tiffany ran out of the room and went downstairs. They escaped the house for a while. Daniel was scared. Although what he had done was Tiffany's plan, he was the one who put it into action. Tiffany, on the other hand, was on cloud nine. She had finally achieved her goal of humiliating Amber.

"There's nothing to be scared of, Daniel. I didn't record your face. It's all right, so don't worry," Tiffany reassured him as they watched the house from a distance. They were waiting for Amber to leave so they could go back inside the house.

Upstairs, Amber was still in shock at what had happened to her. She felt numb. She could not even cry and went about picking up her clothes from the floor. She put them on slowly and then went downstairs, feeling horrible and scared. She ran outside the house and threw up in Tiffany's yard. She started to walk home, filled with sadness and shame at what had just happened to her. First her father and now Daniel.

She reached home and as soon as she went inside, she stumbled to the floor, too weak to stand up any longer. She called out to Jane to help her and Jane came running from the kitchen. She had heard the door close and knew that it meant Amber was back.

Looking at the state Amber was in, Jane quickly understood that something bad had happened to her. She sat beside Amber and hugged her, asking her to calmly tell what had happened.

Amber recounted the whole incident and told Jane how Tiffany had videotaped everything. Jane's blood ran cold as she heard the story. She couldn't believe someone could be so cruel.

CHAPTER 6

JANE COMFORT AMBER

"I'm going to the school Monday morning and speaking to the principal. I will make sure Tiffany's parents also know about it!" Jane said as she helped Amber to her room. She helped Amber undress and into the shower and then she left to give Amber some privacy.

Amber started to scrub herself with soap and continued until she could not scrub herself anymore. She cried a lot, praying to have the strength to move on from the hurt and pain.

She finally got out of the shower and Jane was there with a clean pair of pajamas. She helped Amber get dressed and then tucked her in bed like a child. Jane switched off the light of the room and sat beside Amber till she fell asleep. All that time, Jane prayed to God to help Amber heal from her pain.

The next morning, Jane called Amber downstairs to have some breakfast. Although Amber didn't want to eat anything, Jane would not let her starve herself. Jane reached out and hugged her. She told Amber that everything will be all right and Amber just needs to trust God. Jane also asked Amber to come to the church to pray and Amber agreed.

After breakfast, the two women drove to the church. Richard was already there, waiting for them both. They entered the church together and Amber saw a few people sitting inside. They were busy in prayers but stopped when they heard the Pastor come in. They all gathered at the altar and the pastor led them in prayer.

Everyone held hands and prayed for each other. Just then, Jane told Amber to shout out and praise the Lord. Amber did as asked and she received the Holy Ghosts. All of a sudden, she started to speak in tongues. Everyone around her was astonished but Jane and Richard were happy for her. Once the prayer was over, everyone left soon. Amber, Jane, and Richard also left but instead of going home, Richard took them to a restaurant.

Amber was finally feeling a bit better and had ordered a hearty meal. That's when she heard her phone ring. It was a text from Tiffany. Amber opened her phone and saw the video that Tiffany had recorded in her room.

Horrified, Amber excused herself to go to the restroom and asked Jane to come with her. She showed the video to Jane once they were in the restroom and Amber felt the same creep up on her again.

Jane was upset too but she asked Amber to be patient and they went back to the table. The food arrived soon but both had lost their appetite. Richard asked them if everything was okay and they both just nodded.

They finally reached home and Amber asked Jane to come to her room.

"Have you told the pastor about this?" Amber asked as soon as Jane walked into her room.

Jane hugged her and said, *"I haven't, dear, but we'll have to tell him soon."*

Amber just nodded, knowing well that there was no way they could hide it from Richard.

So, the next day, as the three sat down for dinner, Jane nodded to Amber and she nodded back. Jane understood and as soon as Richard finished eating, she told him about the incident. He was shocked and didn't even know what to say. He suddenly understood why Amber had been on edge the previous day and he just walked away. Jane knew he needed to think about it and reassured Amber that everything was okay.

Jane asked Amber to go and rest, but Amber insisted on helping her clear away the dishes. Soon, they were done, and Jane kissed Amber goodnight before going into her room. Amber too wanted to rest but she was curious to know what Richard thought. So, she slowly walked up to the bedroom and stood listening at the door.

She heard Richard talking about his past and how his sister was also raped by her boyfriend.

"Amber reminds me of my sister, Jane. I still can't forgive myself for not being able to help her."

"Honey, it is not your fault you didn't know and besides, you were just ten years old when that happened to your sister," Jane replied in a soft voice.

Amber heard everything and she ran to her room crying. All this time, she had thought she was the only one going through so much in her life. Listening to the pastor's conversation made her realize that she was not alone. The thought brought some

peace to her mind and for the first time in weeks, Amber slept peacefully.

Sunday morning arrived and Amber got ready for church. The three got in the car after breakfast and drove silently. Amber had joined the Sunday school and Jane was the teacher, so she enjoyed it.

The school started after Mass and Jane started with psalms chapter 56- 1- 8. Amber got lost in the words of the Lord and felt at peace. When Sunday school was over, Amber saw Tiffany's parents and Tiffany sitting in the back row.

Amber was kinda, of mad and sad about what Tiffany had done to her, but she knew the only way to move forward in life was to forgive. She knew, she had to forgive herself and Tiffany and be the bigger person.

The Sunday service began and everybody at church was shouting and praising the Lord. Just then, Amber received the Holy Ghosts again. Tiffany, who was keeping an eye on Amber, got scared because she had never seen anything like that. She clutched her mother's hand until the episode ended.

The pastor came on and preached about forgiveness. He also shared the story about his sister, making everyone teary-eyed. Amber, who could feel his pain too well, started crying. Meanwhile, Tiffany, who was on a guilt trip excused herself and ran to the restroom to get away.

After the service was over, many people came and thanked Richard for the great service. Jane, on the other hand, had her eyes on Tiffany's parents and as soon as she saw them walking towards the church door, she walked towards them briskly.

"Hi. Are you Tiffany's parents? I'm Jane, the pastor's wife. I'd like to have a word with you both," Jane said.

Mr. and Mrs. Dalton stopped in their tracks and turned to greet Jane.

"How can we help you," Mr. Dalton asked.

Jane took a deep breath and told them the whole story, ending with the events at Tiffany's birthday party. As expected, the two didn't believe her and got angry.

"How can you say something like that about our daughter?" Mrs. Dalton exclaimed angrily.

Amber saw the commotion and quickly approached Jane to stop her. But it was no use. Jane had decided enough was enough, and she wanted to put an end to Amber's pain.

"Amber is a really sweet girl. She has been going through some heartache and pain, but I've never heard her complain. Your daughter Tiffany, on the other hand, has everything in life, and still, she tried to ruin Amber's. Tiffany made her boyfriend rape Amber and even recorded it!"

Not wanting to believe a word Jane was saying, Tiffany's parents turned around to Tiffany and asked her to tell the truth. Tiffany started to cry and just nodded. They stared at her in disbelief as Mrs. Dalton slapped Tiffany and said, *"I don't want you in my house anymore."*

Mr. Dalton was also shocked, but he knew what to do. *"From now on you are staying at your grandparent's house. We don't want you in our house, so don't come back!"*

With these words, the two left, leaving Tiffany to cry at the church door.

"*Do* you want to press charges on Tiffany and Daniel?" Jane asked but she already knew the answer.

Amber shook her head, still feeling sorry for Tiffany. Jane could see that too, but she knew Tiffany needed to learn her lesson. So, they also left and were soon home.

Amber tried to put the events at the church at the back of her mind because she wanted to surprise Jane. It was her birthday and Amber had decided to cook season rice, pork, and some potato salad for the family. She set the table after making the food and even got a bottle of Hawaii punch drink.

Richard was in on the plan and was in charge of keeping Jane out of the way. Once Amber was done, she asked both of them to come into the kitchen. Richard had blindfolded Jane and only removed it when she was standing in front of the laden table.

Richard and Amber yelled *"Happy birthday"* as Jane took off the blindfold. She saw the effort Amber had put into the surprise and couldn't help but hug her.

The family sat down to have dinner and they loved the food. Jane was astonished that Amber knew how to cook.

"My mother taught me. And today, I missed her," Amber said with a sad smile.

"She'd be really happy to know how brave her daughter is," Jane said as she hugged Amber again.

After dinner, Amber cleaned up everything and did not let Jane help her. Soon she was in bed, tired out from the day's events. It had been a long day, but she slept peacefully again.

Amber woke up late the next day and rushed down to make breakfast. But Jane was already there and had made Amber's favorite breakfast as a treat for her. Amber smiled at Jane and quickly gobbled down her breakfast.

"Now, don't forget to come straight here in the afternoon after school because we have to go by your father's house today," Jane said.

Amber had forgotten about it, but she nodded and kissed Jane before dashing out the door. As soon as she walked into her school, she saw everyone.

CHAPTER 7

EVERYTHING TURNS OUT GREAT FOR AMBER BUT FOR TIFFANY NOT THAT ALL GREAT

As she walked into her school, she saw everyone looking at Tiffany. Some people were sniggering, while others had disgusted looks on their faces. A few even called her ugly and stupid.

Amber felt bad for Tiffany. She knew that it was Tiffany who had betrayed her but still. Everybody in the school was avoiding her, and even her friends changed their paths when they saw Tiffany approaching. Even Daniel walked past her without even saying hello.

Amber realized that Tiffany had nobody by her side. As soon as Tiffany walked into the classroom, everyone started calling her sick and nasty. Everybody was laughing at her and finally, Tiffany ran out of the classroom in tears. Amber wanted to go after her, but the teacher entered, and the class started.

Amber kept looking for Tiffany and even tried to locate her at lunchtime, but she was nowhere to be seen. Amber was alone at a table, having her lunch when Tiffany's friend Jennifer approached her.

"I'm sorry for treating you horribly in school. Tiffany made me do it but I know it's my fault too and I apologize for it," Jennifer said sincerely.

Jennifer also told Amber that it was her idea to expose Tiffany to everyone in the school. Amber was shocked and asked Jennifer why.

"She told my parents about my drinking problem. She does deserve this. She was not only mean to you, but she was mean to her friends and even her boyfriend. She was just using Daniel to get what she wanted. She doesn't care about us, she was just jealous of you and wanted to make your life miserable," Jennifer said.

"Thank you for helping me out, Jennifer," Amber said before heading back to her classes.

The rest of the day passed peacefully, and Amber decided not to look for Tiffany anymore. She deserved all that had happened to her.

After school, Amber reached home, changed, and then accompanied Jane and Richard to her father's house. They knocked on the door and he opened it, looking healthy and clean. As soon as he saw Amber, he gave her a big kiss on the cheek and invited them into the house.

The house was clean, and everything was in its place. It had a woman's touch and Amber realized that her father must be dating.

Just then a woman walked out of the kitchen and her father introduced her as his wife-to-be. They all sat in the living room and Richard told Amber's father their plan to adopt Amber.

Her father thought for a while and then agreed to sign the paperwork, saying that he wants the best life for Amber.

With tears in his eyes, he said, "*I know haven't been the perfect father in your life. I have made mistakes and I'm not proud of it. Your mother and I would like for you to have a better life. And Amber,*" he said with shame apparent on his face, "*I'm so sorry for what I did to you. I was drinking and got so caught up about the situation with your mom, I didn't know how to heal, till you left me.*"

Listening to these sincere words from her father, Amber started to cry and said, "*I forgive you, Dad.*"

The words took off the heavyweight from her chest and she finally felt free of the guilt and the shame that had been building up inside her. Her father signed the paperwork and Richard got up from the couch to give him a big hug.

Jane and Richard soon went to wait for Amber in the car, while Amber stayed behind to say goodbye to her father. Her father apologized again and said, "*I'm sorry Amber. You deserve so much more; you are a special child. Don't you ever forget that?*"

The father and daughter hugged and said goodbye to each other. Soon, she was on her way home, with Jane and Richard.

Amber's new life started and she was finally happy. Her academics improved too. She was on the honor roll of her class and also got a new friend. Her friend liked her for who she was and was always kind to her. They stayed together all through school and even graduated together.

Amber applied and got accepted by the top colleges in the world. Her friend gets accepted at Stanford University college and both are achieving great things in their careers.

As for Tiffany, she went into the last school of her choice and now she is working a full-time job as a business administrator.

Tiffany's story was sad, hurtful, and upsetting, but after all this, Tiffany learned and grew a lot in her life. Now she knows that her low self-esteem made her mean to others around her.

Amber's life taught her that no matter how much your life gets rough, you have to keep moving. The only people who succeed in this game called life are the ones who develop thick skin. Life may not always be easy but it is up to you to make your own life beautiful.

Today, my message for you is that please don't be disappointed or discouraged when hard times come by. Sometimes life teaches us valuable lessons to make us stronger and we can learn a lot from them. I know you might feel upset and question your fate but know that it all will get better soon.

It is easy to look at the lives of other people and compare them with yours. But we never know what they are going through. They may have a smile on their face, but it doesn't mean they are always happy.

I am thankful for all the blessings in my life and focus on my goals. Trust me that later on in life, you will get the things you only dream of today. But first, you have to heal and let go of the past. If you truly want to be free, stop being frustrated and live your life. I hope you enjoyed this book and it helps you in your life and situation. Just remember you are blessed, and God loves you. May God bless you on your journey.

SELF LOVE POEM

My skin lit up the building like red roses
My skin is priceless
My skin is worth it
My skin is golden
My skin is precious
My skin is like a clock that goes on and on and on.

Love yourself
Love your skin
Love your body
Love your mind
Love your spirit
Love your soul.

Your respect is important
Your confidence is important
Your self-esteem is important
Your responsibilities are important
Your relationship with God is important
Your values are important
Overcoming obstacles is important
Being humble is important

Setting boundaries is important.
Embrace yourself to be free
Embrace yourself with joy
Embrace your life to fulfill your destiny
Embrace the real you inside
Embrace freedom
Embrace your inner healing
Embrace your confidence
Embrace your strength
Embrace your skin.
Pull your mind away from negativity
Pull your mind away from depression
Pull your mind away from anxiety
Pull your mind away from the past
Pull your mind away from the hurt
Pull your mind to a higher level
Pull your mind to a positivity
Pull your mind to a humble
Pull your mind to heal.
Let go of fear
Let go of your ego
Let go of the situation
Let go of the pain
Let go of guilt
Let go of regret
Let go of disappointment
Let go of toxic people
Let go of stress,
Let go and be free

Let go and be happy.
Love
Love yourself
Love your skin!
Let go and let it happen
Embrace your skin
Love your skin!
Embrace your style
Embrace your empowerment
Embrace your loyalties
Embrace yourself!
Fear is not winning
Fear is not a part of you
Fear is not real
Fear is only to chase us away
We are not born with fear
We are born with strength and hope
Don't let fear control you
Beat the fear
Be fearless
Be natural
Be careful.
Be free
Be the one to fulfill your dreams
Keep being positive
Be brave
Be brave to chase your dreams
Be brave to do what you have to do
Be brave to speak up

Be brave, be braver
Let life take you there
No more crying
No more pain.

No more downfalls
No more feeling bad for yourself
No more of 'I'm not good enough. Believe that you are!
No more worrying
No more stress
No more staying with toxic people
No more stopping your blessings
It is time to heal yourself
It's time to heal your situation
It's time to shine.
It's time to take the risk
It's time to go for what you want
It's time to get out of your comfort zone
It's time to be free
It is time to set yourself free
Don't be stuck
Don't be stuck doing the same thing
Don't be stuck in a hole
Don't be stuck in the past
Be your light
Be your sunlight.
Be the woman or man that you like being.
Embrace your feelings
Embrace what you are feeling inside

Don't hold yourself back
Be your boss
Take control of your life
And if you can't take control of your life give it to God
Find yourself again
Find hope again
Find love within you again.
Find courage again
Find faith again.
Find God again
Find me again
See yourself doing big things
See yourself being free
See yourself being positive
See yourself being humble
See yourself being there
See yourself moving up
See yourself being married one day.
See yourself being in a big house
See yourself with your husband
See yourself with your children
See yourself never losing hope
See yourself breaking through obstacles
See yourself being who you truly are
See yourself motivating people
See yourself not being a loser
See yourself being successful
See yourself doing just fine in life
See yourself doing better.

See yourself being strong
See yourself being a survivor
Embrace your happiness
Embrace the joy in you
Embrace the new year
And say,
My skin is flawless
My skin is elegant
My skin is beautiful
My skin is my definition
Skin is so bright and special.
Skin so golden and glittery
Skin so strong and defined
Skin so healthy and soft
Skin so purified and blessed
Skin so grounded and refresh
Skin so raw and unique
It's ok to be different
It's ok to be weird
It's ok to have faith in God
It's ok to be strong
It's ok to have peace.
It's ok to be loved.
It's ok to put yourself first
It is ok that you are loving yourself
It's ok that you want peace in your life
It's ok to do the right thing
It's ok to have fun

It's ok to be free
It's ok to open up
It's ok to do you
It's ok to live a healthy better life
It's oh to be ok.

MY PRAYER

Dear God, as I Come forth to you today. Whoever is stuffed from depression, guilt, low self-esteem, pain, loneliness, or the last of guidance, and feels like the world is against them, I pray and rebuke that spirit in the name of Jesus. As you say, lord, you will never leave us nor forsake us, 'O God let your people know that they're not alone, show them the way of the truth and the light, 'O God. Lord, I thank you for what blessing you have restored for us. That we desire to choose you forever, in the name of Jesus, I pray amen.

WRITE HOW YOU FEEL, EXPRESS YOURSELF

www.ingramcontent.com/pod-product-compliance
Lightning Source LLC
LaVergne TN
LVHW051911060526
838200LV00004B/91